D1402556

Animal World

Snakes

Donna Bailey and Christine Butterworth

STECK-VAUGHN
LIBRARY
A Division of Steck-Vaughn Company

Many people don't like snakes.
They think snakes are cold and slimy.
If you touch the skin of a snake,
you will find that it feels
smooth, cold, and dry.

A snake's skin has many small scales.
When a snake gets bigger,
its skin splits.
Underneath the snake has grown
a new skin.
The snake crawls out of its old skin and
leaves it on the ground.

Most snakes have eyes on the sides
of their heads.
That helps them see around them.
Snakes cannot close their eyes.
Even when snakes are asleep,
their eyes stay open.

Snakes cannot see very well.
Their eyes only tell them when
something nearby is moving.
They cannot hear either because
they have no ears.

When a snake's head is on the ground,
it can feel the ground shake.
It knows when an animal comes close.
This snake can feel the toad coming near.

The toad is afraid of the snake.
It hopes the snake will go away.
When a snake is afraid, it curls up and
pretends to be dead.

A snake uses its forked tongue
to smell the scent of animals.
It flicks it in and out to taste the air.
Can you see the forked tongue
of this snake?

8

A snake's bottom jaw has a hinge, which
helps the snake open its mouth very wide.
It can swallow things which are very large.
Look at this snake swallowing an egg!

The snake can swallow the egg whole.
A sharp bone inside the snake's stomach
breaks the egg.
The snake eats the yolk and the white.
Then it spits out the broken shell.

Many snakes mate in the spring.
The female snake finds a warm nest,
where she lays her eggs after mating.
A snake's nest needs to be in a warm
place so the eggs can hatch.

Snake eggs do not have hard shells.
When the baby snake has grown big
enough to come out of the egg, it breaks
the egg with a special egg tooth.
The egg tooth falls off when
the snake gets out of the shell.

Some snakes, like this adder,
do not lay eggs.
Baby adders are born
in little bags of skin.
They push the bags open with their noses.

Mother snakes do not look after
their babies.
Baby snakes must find their own food
as soon as they are born.

14

The young snakes must
watch for their enemies.
This hawk is hoping to catch
a baby snake.

The colors of snakes help protect them.
This snake has a beautiful pattern
on its skin.
The pattern helps it hide
from enemies.

16

Look at the patterns and colors on
the skin of this coral snake.
They help the snake warn its enemies
to keep away.
The coral snake is very shy, but
if it bites you, it is very poisonous.

Snakes have different ways
of killing their prey.
Some snakes, such as these rattlesnakes,
kill animals by injecting poison into them.

Can you see the poison fangs
of this rattlesnake?
The poison is stored in the hollow fangs.
If the rattlesnake loses a poison fang,
it grows another one in its place.

When the snake attacks its prey,
it opens its mouth wide, and
the poison fangs in front flick forward.
The snake bites its prey and
injects the poison into it.

A rattlesnake can hunt for food
in the dark.
It has two small pits on its face.
These pits can feel heat
from an animal's body.

When the rattlesnake gets ready
to bite its prey, it shakes
the bony rings at the end of its tail.
They make a rattling noise.

Rattlesnakes live in deserts.
In the winter when the desert gets cold,
the rattlesnakes make a den underground.
The rattlesnakes will sleep in
the same den all winter.

This snake is a boomslang.
It lives in trees and
catches lizards and birds to eat.

24

The boomslang has teeth
at the back of its mouth.
It catches an animal and
holds it in its jaws.
Then the snake uses its back teeth
to inject poison to kill the animal.

This green tree python has long front teeth.
It catches birds that fly
among the branches of a tree.

A cobra is a poisonous snake, too.
When a cobra is afraid, it raises
its head and opens its hood
to frighten its enemies.
It can spit poison into your eyes
from six feet away.

This banded sea snake is even
more poisonous than a cobra.
It lives in the warm sea around
the coast of hot countries.
It feeds on fish.

Many snakes are not poisonous.
They kill their prey by squeezing it
so hard that it cannot breathe.
A snake that squeezes like this
is called a constrictor.

This Indian python has wrapped its body
around a deer and is swallowing it whole.
Such a large meal means the python
will not need food for weeks.

This big snake is an anaconda.
It grows up to 25 feet long.
It feeds on birds and animals and
eats them whole.

Pythons and anacondas are both
constrictors.
They kill their prey by squeezing it hard.
They are the biggest snakes in the world.
Look at this giant python fighting
a crocodile!

Index

Reading Consultant: Diana Bentley
Editorial Consultant: Donna Bailey
Supervising Editor: Kathleen Fitzgibbon

Illustrated by Paula Chasty
Picture research by Suzanne Williams
Designed by Richard Garratt Design

Photographs
Cover: Bruce Coleman/(Jane Burton)
Bruce Coleman: 6 (George McCarthy), 7 and 12 (Jane Burton), 9 (John Visser),
    10 and 17 (Michael Fogden), 16 (C. B. and D. W. Frith), 18 (Jeff Foott),
    22 (J. Cancalosi), 23 (David C. Houston), 24 and 25 (Mark Boulton), 28
    (Allen Power), 29 (Frans Lanting), 30 (Gunter Ziesler), 31 (M. Timothy
    O'Keefe)
Frank Lane Picture Agency: 11 (A. R. Hamblin), 32 (Tor Allen)
Eric and David Hosking: title page
NHPA: 8 and 19 (Stephen Dalton), 26 (Ralph & Daphne Keller),
    27 (Anthony Bannister)
OSF Picture Library: 2 (Animals Animals/Z. Leszcynski), 3 (Animals Animals/E. R.
    Degginger), 13 (Tony and Sheila Phelps)

Library of Congress Cataloging-in-Publication Data: Bailey, Donna. Snakes / Donna Bailey and Christine Butterworth:
[illustrated by Paula Chasty]. p. cm. — (Animal world) SUMMARY: Discusses snakes in general and introduces a variety of
specific snakes. ISBN 0-8114-2636-X 1. Snakes—Juvenile literature. [1. Snakes.] I. Butterworth, Christine. II. Chasty, Paul
ill. III. Title. IV. Series: Animal world (Austin, Tex.) QL666.06B18 1990 597.96—dc20 89-26078 CIP AC

2 3 4 5 6 7 8 9 LB 96 95 94 93 92 91 90